BIRDWATCHERS

A play in one act

by

B. A. Hite

Published By
Havescripts

BIRDWATCHERS Copyright ©, B. A. HITE. 2006
All rights reserved.

CAUTION: Professionals and amateurs are hereby warned that performance of BIRDWATCHERS is subject to payment of a royalty unless written permission is given waiving such fee. The Play is fully protected under the copyright laws of the United States of America, and of all countries covered by the International Copyright Union (including the Dominion of Canada and the rest of the British Commonwealth), and of all countries covered by the Pan-American Copyright Convention, the Universal Copyright Convention, and the Berne Convention, and of all countries with which the United States has reciprocal copyright relations. All rights, including professional/amateur stage rights, motion picture, recitation, lecturing, public reading, radio broadcasting, television, video or sound recording, all other forms of mechanical or electronic reproduction, such as CD-ROM, CD-I, DVD, information storage and retrieval systems and photo-copying, and the rights of translation into foreign languages, are strictly reserved. Particular emphasis is placed upon the matter of readings, permission for which must be secured from the Author in writing. Anyone receiving permission to produce the Play is required to give credit to the Author as sole and exclusive Author of the Play on the title page of all programs distributed in connection with performances of the Play and in all instances in which the title of the Play appears for purposes of advertising, publicizing or otherwise exploiting the Play and/or a production thereof. Author's name must be one-third the size of the title.

All rights reserved. Copyright 2006, B. A. Hite

All performances for any audience (classroom/auditorium/paying/nonpaying) must have applied for a performance license and paid performance fees in advance of production.

CAUTION: Professionals and amateurs are hereby warned that performance of BirdWatchers, hereinafter known as Play, is subject to payment of a royalty unless written permission is given waiving such fee. The Play is fully protected under the copyright laws of the United States of America, and of all countries covered by the International Copyright Union (including the Dominion of Canada and the rest of the British Commonwealth), and of all countries covered by the Pan-American Copyright Convention, the Universal Copyright Convention, and the Berne Convention, and of all countries with which the United States has reciprocal copyright relations. All rights, including professional/amateur stage rights, motion picture, recitation, lecturing, public reading, radio broadcasting, television, video or sound recording, all other forms of mechanical or electronic reproduction, such as CD-ROM, CD-I, DVD, information storage and retrieval systems and photo-copying, and the rights of translation into foreign languages, are strictly reserved. Particular emphasis is placed upon the matter of readings, permission for which must be secured from the Author in writing.

Digital versions cannot be added to a free or paid online library or website, in any format, with or without member access without the publisher's permission.

No changes in the script are permitted without written permission by the publisher or playwright. Making changes in a published play without permission is a violation of Federal copyright law, punishable fine and/or imprisonment. For permission please email Blue Moon Plays at info@bluemoonplays..com.

Publisher: Blue Moon Plays
Blue Moon Plays, LLC
1385 Fordham Road, Ste 105-279
Virginia Beach, VA 23464
Printed in the USA
ISBN# 978-1-943416-85-1

CHANGES TO SCRIPT

Copyright law prevents this script from being copied or altered in any way by any technical or digital means. There may be no changes made to the script including but not limited to casting or dialogue without permission of the publisher and/or playwright.

No changes in the script are permitted without written permission by the publisher or playwright. Making changes in a published play without permission is a violation of Federal copyright law. For permission please email Blue Moon Plays at info@bluemoonplays..com.

PERFORMANCE/READING OF SCRIPT

This script is licensed for production by blue moon plays. It may NOT be performed or read aloud in any way (with or without admission fees) in a classroom, around a table, in front of a non-paying audience without a performance fee, which varies.

For any performance, you must apply for and purchase performance rights: in class, in school, for educational purposes, for paying or nonpaying audiences of any size, as a concert reading or a staged reading.

Anyone receiving permission to produce the Play is required to give credit to the Author as sole and exclusive Author of the Play on the title page of all programs distributed in connection with performances of the Play and in all instances in which the title of the Play appears for purposes of advertising, publicizing or otherwise exploiting the Play and/or a production thereof. Author's name must be one-half the size of the title.

Special Considerations:

Small-group readings around a table or in the classroom:
- If you are planning to use this script FOR CLASSROOM USE, you must purchase scripts for the members of your class or group. These may be purchased as a downloadable PDF (class/group study pack) which may be printed for that class only.
- If you are a small group doing private play readings for YOUR OWN ENTERTAINMENT or for a SMALL SENIOR ACTIVITY GROUP, you must purchase the number or scripts required by the characters: these may be purchased as a multi-copy download which will give you a printable script that you may copy for that reading only.

Video Taping
One video tape may be made for archival purposes only.

Livestreaming
Livestreaming is permissible with an additional fee.

Digital versions cannot be added to a free or paid online library or website, in any format, with or without member access, without the publisher's permission.

TO PERFORM THIS PLAY

You must buy sufficient scripts for the cast + 3, apply for performance rights, pay the performance fee, and receive a performance license.

To purchase scripts:
- Purchase sufficient printed hard copies (one for each cast member, plus 3 for the crew) - an automatic 10 percent discount is applied to multiple printed hardcopies at the point of ordering.

or

- Purchase a Multicopy PDF which allows you to print sufficient copies of this script (one for each cast member, plus 3 for the crew). Click Return to Merchant to download your printable PDF. A link to the download will also be emailed to you, along with a link to the application for performance license.

To apply for a Performance License, go to the Product Page of the play and fill out and submit the application form.

To pay the Performance Fee, simply pay the invoice you will be emailed when we receive your application for performance.

Your Performance License for your requested dates will be emailed to you.

All scripts and licenses shall be obtained at Blue Moon Plays at www.havescripts.com

If you wish to make changes in the script of any kind, you must receive permission from the publisher or the playwright. Permission is usually granted readily when schools or theaters face casting problems and the changes do not affect the quality or intent of the original

BIRDWATCHERS

CHARACTERS:
HE, a free lance writer.

SHE, a birdwatcher.

SCENE: A forest clearing.

TIME: The Present

(HE comes in with much equipment—folding chair, binoculars, two cameras, safari hat. and thermos of martinis—sets up his stuff, pours a drink, begins scanning the area with binoculars. SHE comes in. sets up her stuff—campstool. binoculars, camera, large purse—begins scanning the area with binoculars. They discover each other through the binoculars.)

SHE: *(Pause.)* Hi there!
HE: Hey... there...
SHE: Are you... ? That is to say... were you... ?
HE: What?
SHE: Well, that is. .. Are we here... both here... both to be...?
HE: To be...?
SHE: ... doing the same thing? Both here to - come here to... are you... here to...
HE: Here to. .. ?
SHE: Are you by any chance doing the same thing

I'm doing?
HE: I have no idea.
SHE: Well, I mean to say, that is, one doesn't expect to find another... one... sitting in a certain spot in the forest... *(Pause.)*... Someone who's not fishing or picnicking... So I was merely wondering if...
HE: I see.
SHE: Wondering if -
HE: *(Cutting in.)* I'm out here to see a bird, a certain ivory-billed woodpecker, almost extinct, rumored to be building -
SHE: That's it! Imagine! According to the Audubon Journal a pair of ivory-billed woodpeckers are building their nest right here in this very forest! In this very area!
HE: Well, I'm sure glad for the official information.
SHE: Then you must be my partner.
HE: What?
SHE: My pair, uh... my partner...
HE: I didn't know we were supposed to have partners.
SHE: Oh, yes, for verification.
HE: Oh, "verification." Well, I don't know. Maybe I am, then.
SHE: Good. Right. *(Rises.)* Let's set up our station! *(Crosses to shake hands.)* I'm Alice Wren.
HE: *(Extending hand.)* Martin Field.
SHE: I'm so happy to meet you. Now, we want to move our things together just a little bit. We'll confine our area more that way. *(Going to get stool.)* Of course, this is not what you'd call a

regulation field station, but for lack of anything else to call it, I always call it that.
HE: Oh. Oh, we can call it that. Really.

SHE: Right. Well now. Good. So, out with the equipment. *(Goes to her spot. gets stuff. Pause, watching him.)* You were assigned to this location?
HE: Well, no, not that I know of. It just seemed like a likely spot. Shady, not too shady. Quiet. It wasn't that I had any particular kind of spot in mind beforehand. I was looking for a spot and when I got here, I thought this seemed like a good one.
SHE: But do your have your card?
HE: My card?
SHE: Your Audubon card, for identification.
HE: Oh. No, I don't. I just heard... this morning... you know, spur of the moment.
SHE: *(Standing, laughs a bit.)* Oh, it's easy to forget on the spur of the moment. Well... *(Setting up.)* I don't suppose it matters this time... about the card. *(Pause. Watches, then :)* I'll bet this is your first experience.
HE: Yeah. That's right. First time out!
SHE: Well, you're going to really enjoy it, I'm sure. *(Goes to sit.)*
HE: Yep. I didn't know what to bring along in the way of equipment, you know.

(Indicating all his stuff. Sits.)

SHE: Right. I think we always feet so much more

at home with some of our own things around
us. *(Pause. She gets tissue for nose.)*
HE: Are you native to this area, Miss... Finch?
SHE: Wren... No, no. Wren... Alice Wren.
HE: *(Laughing, overlapping her correction.)* Oh, I'm sorry.
SHE: *(Also laughing.)* It's all right. People often get it confused. Yes, I was born 'n raised... just down the road.

(Pause. SHE gets book out. marks page.)

HE: What's that book you have there?
SHE: Oh, this? Oh, it's just my official Audubon Field Guide. I'm afraid not to use it. On the only occasion I ever used something else, I had a terrible time getting confirmation.
HE: *(After a pause.)* What... uh... what kind of confirmation do you get?
SHE: Well, you confirm that you've actually seen the bird you think you've seen.
HE: Oh, yeah, yeah. *(SHE gets camera out. Loads it. Pause.)* I hope you don't feel... inhibited, that I'm here, too.
SHE: Oh, no, not at all. I'm used to it really.
HE: Ah.
SHE: You know, I... I once almost got a picture of a fly catcher about to... *(opens mouth, indicates.)*
HE: Catch a fly?
SHE: Just about! *(She looks away and wipes camera.)*
HE: I could move to the other side of the tree.

SHE: Now don't be silly. This is a pastime that one thinks of as being secluded or, well, solitary. Secluded is not a word that seems to fit with our pastime, is it? A secluded pastime sounds odd. Say rather a solitary sort of activity. You yourself made reference to that fact before when you spoke of the quiet. Yes, one does expect to be quiet at a time like this. *(Rises, goes left.)* But according to the regulations, two are necessary for verification and, actually, to be perfectly honest, I wouldn't know what to think if I were doing it alone. *(Looks down and up.)* Although I've never been paired with a man before.
HE: I was afraid of that. I was afraid I'd make you nervous.
SHE: If we're partners, I don't think we should question it. No one wants to feel out of place and no one is. I think you just have to accept that. You can question anything, you know.
HE: Like who belongs and who might not?
SHE: We want to remember why we're here.
HE: Then you're not concerned about the matter of the card.
SHE: Of course I'm concerned about the matter of the card, but I'm sure you have an explanation for that. *(She waits.)*
HE: *(Pause.)* Have you, uh... have you always been interested in birds. Miss... Wren?
SHE: I've always loved all living things really. I always had a little turtle or fish around. *(Awkward pause.)* Well... and what about you? Were you, too, an animal-lover from the very

first?
HE: Oh, I'm a writer.
SHE: Really, how exciting!
HE: You might say I exaggerate my interests.
SHE: Oh, through imagination! That's wonderful.
HE: Yeah.

(Awkward pause. SHE gets camera, rises.)

SHE: Well, let's see. I'm just going to try to get my bearings. I like to take a few shots of the general area before things start... happening.

(Looking through camera.)

HE: The setting. That's a good idea, background material.

SHE: *(Clicking, unconsciously posing as she turns.)* I knew a man once who took pictures of the woods and mountains on his vacation and blew them up, you know, enlarged them to cover his entire living room walls when he got home. Isn't that unusual? It was quite an unusual effect.
HE: *(In one of his ways of speaking.)* I can imagine... he said with a curious inflection.
SHE: He only turned them on for parties or dinners... Such a novel idea.
HE: *(Pause. Then:)* A woman is very lovely in the woods.
SHE: *(Pause.)* Are you saying that deliberately to

make me nervous?
HE: No, no, it just seemed like a perfectly normal thing to say.
SHE: *(Turning away.)* We're partners, you know, but that doesn't mean we have to speak. As a rule, it's better to maintain silence anyway.

(She takes out tissue and folds it.)

HE: *(Stands, goes right.)* Wait a minute. You mean to tell me there are couples of absolute strangers sitting in awkward degrees of silent intimacy throughout this entire... forest? Like this?
SHE: I don't think you're ready to sympathize with the situation.
HE: I don't believe it. I think you're making it up.
SHE: Oh, no, no, it's according to the regulations.
HE: Right. Yeah, you seem to be a person who's very careful to know all the rules, do all the right things.
SHE: Yes.
HE: I don't want to start a movement, but the idea makes me want to climb a tree. Just how many... "partners"... do you suppose there are sitting here and there throughout the area in various official positions?
SHE: I see what you mean. You miss the spontaneity.
HE: The seclusion...
SHE: The spirit of primitive discovery...
HE: Yeah... that spirit...
SHE: But you see, there are people who want to

abuse the Natural Resources.
HE: You should talk to some of my friends.
SHE: If we were at a cocktail party, we'd never meet each other.
HE: I don't know.
SHE: Yes, you'd be talking with people in dark glasses and raised eyebrows.
HE: Ha, that's good, or with women who have very few eyebrows and are always paired with a man. (*Pause.*) When I was sixteen I used to imagine I was locked in a prison cell for being a spy. I was locked there with another spy who turned out to be a girl in disguise. A nice girl, hardly talked at all, quiet, very attractive and pure. Very dedicated to the purpose of our mission. We were both scheduled to die for treason. Naturally, we fell in love. It was the only time I saw her reserve break down. Sometimes I saved her and sometimes I saved us both. Sometimes we died together. Prior to that we shared a brief, but meaningful, relationship.
SHE: I used to imagine, too. I imagined I was a wounded nurse in the war, left for dead in the forest. This sensitive soldier finds me and waits with me for help to arrive. He never speaks to me or touches me in an aggressive manner. He is in uniform and very mindful of his duty. But of course we fall in love, too. I am fascinating, even wounded—in my mind I am. It is difficult for him to maintain his duty. It calls for terrific restraint.
HE: It's funny when you're younger.

SHE: Imagination is much easier when you're younger.
HE: Just the opposite for me.
SHE: Oh, for you. I guess you're right! Well, it's never easy.
HE: And you never want to come out of that prison cell.
SHE: To see help arrive and wake up in the hospital with everyone else. *(Pause.)* You know, I think it's out of place to have pictures of woods and mountains all over your living room walls.
HE: It is, he said with raised eyebrows ... Wait!
SHE: What?
HE: Shhh. Don't move. Shhh. *(HE rises, and, looking up. slowly creeps to the side of the stage. SHE follows.)*
SHE: What? Do you see it?
HE: Shhh. Don't move.
SHE: Where? Where is it?
HE: *(Crawls down right, looks, runs around upstage.)* I thought I saw it. We've got to be careful. We're making entirely too much noise.

(They move back toward chairs.)

SHE: I just had a thought. Do you know what I think? I think we're exposing ourselves too much. I think perhaps we should move our position. Under a tree.
HE: You've got a point there. We should be covered up.
SHE: Right. Let's move our things. *(Picks up stool*

    and chair, stops.) Which tree... do you
    think...?
HE: Listen, you've had more experience at this
    thing than I have.
SHE: Well, maybe... there...?
HE: Provided we can see clearly enough...
    (Checks around.) Here?
SHE: Right. I'll just give you a hand with some of
    your things. This is so cozy.

(Pause as they get settled.)

HE: Say, uh, what happens if you have to, you
    know... go to the bathroom?
SHE: Oh. Well. There's a rest room in the
    Information Center at the entrance.
HE: How far is that?
SHE: Didn't you see it?
HE: No.
SHE: Well, it's not far... *(Pause.)* Do you... ?
HE: Oh, no, no; I was just curious. *(They begin
    to look through binoculars. Pause.)*
SHE: *(Whisper.)* You know, it's interesting to watch
    a man doing the same thing you are...
HE: Well, I'm probably not. I'm probably much
    more serious about this than you are...
SHE: What do you mean "serious"?
HE: Serious. My life's work.
SHE: Oh, as a writer you mean.
HE: This may be a matter of my bread and butter,
    whereas for you, some woman's club probably.
    "Girls, Alice Wren is going to devote her entire
    day next Saturday, all day, to getting a glimpse

of our famous ivory-billed, double-breasted woodpecker. What about that, girls?"

SHE; Double-breasted woodpecker. How serious is that?

HE: It's just an attitude.

SHE: *(Standing, crossing behind him)* Logically, I wouldn't want to disturb you if it meant your livelihood, but on the other hand, I hate to be insulted.

HE: My work is very relevant to the World, he said with a careless shrug.

SHE: I bet you're writing a book.

HE: It must be done with the utmost accuracy.

SHE: Men have such special feeling for pages. Line after line... Confronting the world from between the covers. Man speaks to Nature. Nature speaks to Man.

HE: It's not a book.

SHE: Oh, yes, I know what it is! You're doing the movie script first. Right. That's it!

HE: I shouldn't have insulted you.

SHE: *(Crossing to him.)* Wait. I can see a TV series. Backwoods social renegade, perhaps widowed with small, adorable child, battles poachers and politicians to protect the bird he loves. Each episode takes us deeper into the world of real man as he pits himself against the elements of nature. You could have a hurricane one time, and a flood, swamp poison, alligators, Spanish moss...

HE: And a woman who wants him to go to Washington to save the swamp. "But Mary, I'd be like a fish out of water in Washington. The

swamp is my home; it's all I've ever known.
(SHE giggles.') Shhh.
SHE: What?
HE: Don't move.
SHE: What? Again? Where?

HE: Shhh. *(He moves to try to see it. SHE follows.)*
I feel sure I saw a large object... moving... It is a large bird, isn't it? How large a bird is it?
SHE: Eighteen. .. uh. .. oh, I have my book here. *(Crosses to chair, right.)* Let's see. Yes. "Length 18 inches. Red crested head plumage".
HE: I feel sure I saw something of that nature. There...
SHE: Well...
HE: I don't see it now.
SHE: Mmmm.
HE: Maybe we should... *(Indicates chairs.)*
BOTH: Move... over there...
SHE: Maybe you're right. *(They move.)*
HE: *(Pause.)* Here? Let's see... There we go! *(Pause.)* Would you like a drink?
SHE: What?
HE: A drink.
SHE: You really have come prepared! I usually plan ahead to fix up a little iced tea or lemonade or even just some good old plain water to bring, but today I was just so rushed that I -
HE: Martini, dry martini.
SHE: What?
HE: Not only do you get paired with a man, but

then he turns out to be a drunkard...
SHE: I'm sure you know what you're doing.
HE: I wish you'd just go ahead and say what you think.
SHE: I am really. I think we've built up quite an open relationship really.
HE: Do you?
SHE: You're not an ornithologist, are you?
HE: To be truthful, no. I write stories or articles—whatever you want to call them—on various topics, whatever strikes my fancy, or most likely, whatever is available at the moment. Lots of times I have to do some research, if something comes up that I'm not familiar with. Last year I did a piece on canoeing for the Free Sportsman, and I watched these guys make their own canoe and try it out.
SHE: How exciting!
HE: As a matter of fact, I don't need to actually see the bird to write the story. You know, once I get a feel for the setting, I could create the bird in my mind.
SHE: Really? Well, would that be fact or fiction you're writing?
HE: Frankly, you see, there's very little distinction in your popular mags these days. You know, everybody wants his facts jazzed up-turn 'em into an adventure story. Say, for instance, you're doing a thing on infection, pretty scientific, you know. You don't want to say: "Infection results from the presence of certain poisonous micro-organisms in the body ..." Naw, naw... You see, you'd want to grab 'em

up with something like: "There's a battle being waged in the channels of your bloodstream at this very moment. . . In the darkest recesses of the veins... "

SHE: That is much more involving isn't it? I see what you mean.

HE: Now, at the same time, if you're writing fiction, you want to get it to come very down to earth and close to home. Say your main character is a psychopath who's set on destroying an entire city by poisoning the water supply. Well, you want to make him very much like the guy next door, a family man—empties the trash, cuts the lawn, plays catch with the neighborhood kids. You know.

SHE: A surprise ending. I never thought of it like that.

HE: There's a longing for realistic sensationalism in the air... at the breakfast table... orange juice that tastes more like oranges than oranges themselves do. That sort of thing

SHE: Oh. I think I see what you mean. *(Thinking, moving away.)* I was just wondering then, how are you going to do this story?

HE: Well...

SHE: "There was a mysterious air about the forest that morning..."

HE: Hey, good, very good!

SHE: Then what?

HE: *(Thinking.)* I'll describe the forest glen, in detail...

SHE: And then...?

HE: I'll build up suspense by describing a few of

the more common birds of the area...
SHE: Which?
HE: Which?
SHE: *(By him.)* Which birds? Which of the more common birds?
HE: Well, I don't know. I'll have to work that out.
SHE: Maybe you could invent them too.
HE: Of course not. I can just look around, and— What's the matter with you?
SHE: There we are in the mist of the mysterious early morning air, watching the robin hop-hop-hopping along when suddenly we're going to feel the power and glory of the mighty wings winging... schoom! Dipping! And there we all are, in the midst of the great hoax.
HE: That's not true.
SHE: No, it's not. What is it then...?
HE: It goes beyond that, when you read it, beyond truth... as you describe it.
SHE: An extraordinary lie.
HE: Art.
SHE: *(Pause, then closing in.)* Do you know what I bet? I'll bet you don't even have an Auduboncard.
HE: Aha! That's it, is it? I knew it. I knew you were getting at something, trying to wheedle it out. No, I don't have one, and wouldn't have one, wouldn't take it if someone gave it to me, paid me for it. I don't believe in cards or numbers or official positions.
SHE: It's a matter of assuming responsibility for your actions. Being accountable, that's all.

(Looking for her card.)

HE: I don't want any part of it.
SHE: This is an Audubon-protected forest.
HE: I know all about that kind of protection. And you sign a special register, time of entry, time of departure, largest bird observed -
SHE: There are people who take advantage... I can't find it, can't find my card.
HE: Oho!
SHE: I thought it was right here with my Sears Charge plate.
HE: Driver's license, social security. Blue Cross, Blue Shield, Gulf, Exxon, Visa, Master Charge-
SHE: I can't find it.
HE: Illegal! Both illegal! Illegal in the "Audubon-protected forest."
SHE: I hate not to know where something is.
HE: We knew it was wrong, but fate seemed to compel us, held us in a tenacious grip.
SHE: No... no. No Master Card... anymore...
HE: We're both in this thing together, he whispered. Let's neither of us forget that fact for even an instant.
SHE: I charged my whole living room set... last December, and...
HE: Early American?
SHE: What? I just don't see it...
HE: Your living room. Early American?
SHE: Spanish revival. That really upsets me.
HE: Oh. Chachacha.
SHE: *(Realizing.)* Well, that's it, is it? That really makes it clear. I see what you're doing, trying

to pull me down. You didn't want to be partners in the first place.
HE: *(Angry.)* No, I came to look for a bird!
SHE: Oh, that's what you say, that's what you think, but you didn't come to <u>see</u> a bird. You're pretending, you're filling your pad there with pretense, that's the truth! And you're not so much better for it.
HE: I hope to see that bird. I hope to see the bird, not carry on a conversation about someone's imitation living room furniture. *(Angrily moving his chair away from hers).* I have to get a feeling... I came to get a feeling for my story...

(Long pause.)

SHE: But what about me? What will you do with me? In your story. What will you do?
HE: *(Sees her problem)* Oh.
SHE: I'd like to know.
HE: *(Looks at her. Long pause, then:)* Would you want to be in there?
SHE: That would depend...
HE: Would you want to be in there... as you are?
SHE: *(Smiles.)* Oh. Well...
HE: Or...
SHE: I could be something more... sensational. *(Pause.)* Once upon a time... I imagined an enchanted forest... Flowers bloom at the foot of the trees even though the sun never reaches them. *(Change.)* But if you could put me in there... the way I am...

HE: *(Smiles.)* Well, I can see the possibilities -*(HE looks up. sees the bird.)* Wait! Don't move! Slowly... on that oak between the pines there, on the trunk up around the third or fourth branch on the left. See it?
SHE: Yes, yes! ... Oh, it's beautiful, beautiful!
HE: *(Whispering.)* Is it an ivory-billed woodpecker?
SHE: *(Also whispering.)* Oh. I have my confirmation guide... here...

(Gets book.)

HE: Slowly, slowly.
SHE: I have the page marked... here... oh, yes...
HE: Okay. What?
SHE: That must be it. The white...
HE: What does it say?
SHE: "extensive white on wing, folded and in flight, and white bill are diagnostic."—and that means distinguishes it from the pileated woodpecker -
HE: Let's see that thing. Yeah. Yeah. That looks like it. I'll be damned!

(Getting camera, shooting, etc.)

SHE: Oh, it's really exciting. *(Glancing, noticing him.)* My camera! My camera's over there.
HE: *(Taking pictures.)* Never mind. Don't move. I'll send you what I get.

(Kneeling, getting different shots.)

SHE: But... I -
HE: Look! Commit to memory!
SHE: But I just –
HE: *(Gives her a piece of paper.)* Describe it, what it's doing. *(HE begins to write.)*
SHE: Just to see it... so special. *(Change.)* What are you writing?
HE: Descriptions... this and that...
SHE: Descriptions!
HE: I wonder if that stuff sticking out of that hole is the nest. Do you have any information on that?
SHE: Oh. L..

(Starts to look in book then stops.)

HE: Not very neat, is it. All those sticks. Hardly room for the bird.
SHE: Somehow, I hate to think of you... using that bird.
HE: I hate to think of you wasting it.
SHE: *(Louder, rising.)* It's not a waste to let something alone!
HE: Shhh. Let it alone, then. Be quiet.
SHE: It's not a waste to sit and watch.
HE: *(Louder.)* Sit Sat Sat. I call it a waste.
SHE: A liar and exploiter makes that kind of statement, and that is a waste. *(Takes his writing pad.)* That's what's a waste!
HE: Going to club meetings! Learning rules! That is a waste!

(Pokes her pocketbook. speaking louder.)

HE *(contd)*:That is nothing! Means nothing. Nothing. No thing.

(Kicks pocketbook.)

HE *(contd):* Not a thing. Waste. Vanity. Trivia. Bobby-pins and mosaic pillboxes.

SHE: My bird book was in there!
HE: Hateful, shameful waste, pollution, rigmarole, rot. Using some dead animal's hide to carry around a lot of Nothing!
SHE: *(Tearing up his pad.)* Oh, you and your creations and your... your... observations, scraping and picking away at the seams. *(Throwing pages from the pad.)* And your notations, deceiving descriptions... inventions! ...

(Silence. They know the bird is gone. They look up for a count of five or six, then back at each other.)

HE: Well. I guess partners don't usually get so carried away.
SHE*:* *(Weak smile.)* No, they never do.
HE: She said with an enigmatic smile.
SHE: Well. I don't suppose... *(Looks back up.)*
HE: Would it be coming back any time soon...?
SHE: Well, according to... *(Changes, stops.)* No, I'm sure not... *(Pause.)* Not for several - well, not for some hours ... No.

HE: *(Change.)* But we did see it!

(They look back up.)

SHE: Yes, we did! It was beautiful. It was. *(Pause. They look.)*
HE: So. *(Looks back at her.)* It's on the tip of my tongue to say that I enjoyed meeting you, sharing this morning's activities with you.
SHE That's the usual thing to say.
HE: Um... I'll have to think of something... more... something more sensational.
SHE: *(SHE nods.)* You could!
HE: I'll work on that. *(Holds look. Then HE moves to collect some of his papers and to hand her her purse. SHE gives him the pad. SHE gets her purse back in order. Pause.)* In the meantime, don't forget to check in "la casa" for that Audubon card... when you get home.
SHE: Oh, I won't. In "la casa"... *(Smiles.)*
HE: Yeah. Well, so long then.
SHE: So long. *(Pause.)* Goodbye. *(HE goes. SHE waits, then calls after him.)* I'm sorry. *(Lower.)* We lost the bird.

(SHE goes and picks up the campstool. turns, sees some of his papers still on the ground picks them up and almost puts them. unread, in her purse. But the idea of reading them occurs to her and SHE begins to read, coming upon one that SHE reads aloud quietly.)

SHE: "Miss Wren enchants the forest."

(But the problem comes up again, and SHE says. more loudly toward where HE has gone:)

SHE: You! How can anyone believe you?

(SHE puts the paper in her purse, or begins to, then starts to go, looks back, begins to smile; and looking up where the bird was, then where he left, repeats half-seriously:)

SHE:"... enchants the forest... "

(SHE looks up quickly again to where the bird was, smiles, and leaves.)

END OF PLAY

MORE SHORT PLAYS WITH SMALL CASTS

Short Shorts for Seniors by Ludmilla Bollow
This collection contains a variety of short plays for senior citizens. Funny and touching at the same time, these plays illustrate the drama that touches our everyday lives. Includes
FATLESS FUTURE - A Comedy in Five Minutes
 CITY SIDEWALKS - A ten minute one woman monologue
 MOUSSAKA MEETING - A ten minute play
STANLEY & STELLA - A ten minute comedy
SUNSET ZOO -A Ten Minute Comedy/Drama

A Chair: A Senior Comedy by B. A. Hite
An older couple is considering renting an apartment occupied by a "famous" person recently deceased. When the woman finds an old chair she thinks it may have been "his" and therefore, special. Her husband begins to reflect on his own life, wondering what has been special for him. Together, they move to a new place

Plays about Women

The Pinch Hitter: a one act comedy by Jean Klein Set in a domestic household, The Pinch Hitter pokes gentle humor at a woman pushed to the limits by the needs of her family. Her husband is overwhelmed by a new business venture, two of her children are self-absorbed, and her eldest son copes, with her help, with mild mental retardation. As a result, she wears herself out by becoming the pinch hitter for the entire team. It has been produced at the Kempsville Playhouse and the Generic Theater in Virginia and as a finalist in a playwriting competition at the Barn Theater in New Jersey.

The Unmasking of Yetta Breen: by Mickey Coburn A touching and funny "dramady" about a newly widowed middle-aged woman and her changing relationships with her grown children. Yetta's family expect her to remain "mama," dependent and indecisive. Yetta, however, surprises them and herself when the likker salesman arrives. Delightfully entertaining!

She'll Find Her Way Home: a love story of Mound Bayou, Mississippi, in two acts by Valetta Anderson The only child of a wealthy though deceased Mississippi slaveholder, Martha Robb views her coming of age with the expectations of adolescent longings and the seemingly unending horizons promised by the victorious Union Army and her quadroon complexion. She and her lifelong and as fair complexioned friend, Thomas, could forge new lives for themselves, lives without barriers... if they could only get past her mother. But Gussie will not be swayed. Isaiah Montgomery, Vicksburg's newest, wealthiest, coal-black complexioned store owner, is more than welcome to come courting her daughter. "She'll Find Her Way Home" is a fictionalized account of the courtship of Martha and Isaiah Montgomery, the historical founders of the African-American town of Mound Bayou, Mississippi

"Best Always, Marilyn Monroe": a play in two acts by Leslie McBlair "Best Always" is a study of the famous blonde bombshell in what might be called the limited private moments of her life after she became a star. Her life was eerily lonely and filled with long telephone conversations with friends, doctors and strangers. The rest of her days and nights were filled with the business of making films and appearances. This play was a finalist in the 1988 Virginia Prize for Playwriting.

www.ingramcontent.com/pod-product-compliance
Lightning Source LLC
Chambersburg PA
CBHW071804040426
42446CB00012B/2705